I0146643

William E. F Krause

American interests in Borneo

A brief sketch of the extent, climate and productions of the island of B..

William E. F Krause

American interests in Borneo
A brief sketch of the extent, climate and productions of the island of B..

ISBN/EAN: 9783744721400

Printed in Europe, USA, Canada, Australia, Japan

Cover: Foto ©Suzi / pixelio.de

More available books at **www.hansebooks.com**

AMERICAN INTERESTS IN BORNEO.

A BRIEF SKETCH

OF THE

Extent, Climate and Productions

OF THE

ISLAND OF BORNEO.

SECOND EDITION:

WITH AN APPENDIX REDISCUSSING AND PRESENTING NEW VIEWS OF THE
MATTERS UNDER CONSIDERATION.

By WM. E. F. KRAUSE.

SAN FRANCISCO:
H. H. BANCROFT AND COMPANY.
1867.

AMERICAN INTERESTS IN BORNEO.

A BRIEF SKETCH

OF THE

Extent, Climate and Productions

OF THE

ISLAND OF BORNEO.

SECOND EDITION,

WITH AN APPENDIX REDISCUSSING AND PRESENTING NEW VIEWS OF THE
MATTERS UNDER CONSIDERATION.

By WM. E. F. KRAUSE.

SAN FRANCISCO:

H. H. BANCROFT AND COMPANY.

1867.

INTRODUCTORY.

The intelligence recently received through the telegraph, and reliable private sources, that a company of enterprising American capitalists have purchased and secured possession of a large portion of the Island of Borneo, will render a few remarks concerning that important Island interesting to those who have a desire to see our national commerce and influences extended among the rich Islands which skirt the shores of the great Asiatic Continent in the direct line of communication between San Francisco, China and Japan. It is to serve this purpose that this pamphlet has been written by its author.

W. E. F. K.

San Francisco, Cal., March 1st, 1867.

AMERICAN INTERESTS IN BORNEO.

Where is Borneo?

So little is known of this new field for American enterprise, by the generality of people, that when the great
importance of its acquisition is referred to, the question is
usually asked, "Where is Borneo?" For the information
of those who have not paid much attention to the practical
study of geography, it may be stated, that off the southeastern extremity of Asia, and separated from it by the
Chinese Sea, there is a cluster of large, fertile, and thickly
populated islands, which constitute a portion of what in
modern geography is termed Oceanica, or what is better
known, perhaps, as Malaysia. Of all the islands in this
group Borneo is by far the largest; in fact, it is the largest
Island in the world, except Australia. It is situated
directly on the equator. Its greatest length being 778
miles, and greatest width 685 miles, embracing an area
of 316,320 square miles, and stretching from 7° of north
to 4° of south latitude, and from 108° to 119° of east longitude. It is consequently seven times as large as Cuba, or
twice as large as the State of California.

Its History.

As far back as 1526 Borneo was discovered by those
adventurous Portuguese navigators who so greatly ex-

tended European commerce with Asia during the six-
teenth century. But no permanent settlement of Europeans
among its inhabitants was made till 1598, when a small
party of Dutch adventurers, under Van Noort, landed, and
commenced the cultivation of some of the indigenous
productions of the Island, and succeeded so well that in
1664 an extensive trade in spices, ratans, benzoin, sago,
camphor, etc., was carried on between Borneo and Hol-
land. The Dutch pepper plantations furnished a great
portion of the supply for Europe in the seventeenth century. The English, ever jealous of the Dutch progress
in the East, obtained a foothold in Borneo, when an
active rivalry between the two nations commenced, which
injured the·interests of both. The Dutch, by securing a
monopoly of the·pepper trade drove the English out of
the field, and in 1785 obtained from the reigning Sultan a
cession of a portion of the southern division of the Island,
which they retain at this time. The English, aware of
the great importance of the Island in a commercial point
of view, returned,·established themselves, and remained
during the greater part of the eighteenth century; but
owing to the character of a portion of the natives, their
addiction to pillage and piracy; the progress of the rival
settlements was impeded, and the commerce of the Island
dwindled into insignificance, the natives being captured
and sold into slavery. The population decreased more
than one-half within a century, and the Island of Borneo
became almost as much a *terra incognita* as it had been
prior to its discovery by the Portuguese. Its valuable
plantations, forests, and mines ceased to yield any con-
tributions to the commerce of the world, till an accident
induced a young English gentleman, Mr. James Brooke,
to visit the Island in his yacht in 1839. This gentleman,
struck with its amazing natural wealth, and deeply interested in its people, determined to make an attempt to
reclaim the Island and civilize its inhabitants. How well
he has succeeded the increasing importance of the exports

from this Island, and the spread of Christianity, with its
civilizing influences among its inhabitants, are the best
proofs. This gentleman, after years of faithful service in
his self-imposed mission, and the expenditure of a large
fortune for the benefit of the people among whom he has
decided to cast his lot, finally became a Rajah, or Prince,
and was granted a tract of the · richest portion of the
Island. This grant has a. frontage on the sea-coast of
sixty miles, and extending inland some seventy or eighty
miles. ‚It is located on the northeastern extremity of
the Island—the most. salubrious portion. Within the
coast-line of this grant are the mouths of two navigable
rivers,· of much service in furthering the aims of commerce. ·Mr. Brooke,·taking· a deep interest in his Rajah-
ship, has sought every means to bring its importance
before the world; and, being a fine specimen of the Anglo-
Saxon, he has been in favor of going ahead. Having
been treated with indignity by the British Government, to
which he made overtures to cede his possessions, provided
it would aid in developing. its resources and civilizing its
inhabitants, Mr. Brooke has, for years past, been seeking
the aid of Americans to carry out the purpose to which
he has devoted his life and fortune. The recent news
that the northern portion of Borneo, and· some of the
adjacent islands, have been ceded to a company of American capitalists, warrants us in believing that this object·
has at last been attained, and a new field for American
enterprise, of vast extent and importance, has been opened.
To call attention to this fact, we have written these remarks
upon American Interests in Borneo.

ITS RESOURCES.

Owing to its being so near the equator, Borneo is not
adapted for the cultivation of the cereals; but its deep,
rich soil produces in luxurious abundance all the valuable

fruits and woods peculiar to the tropics. Its forests consist of trees, the timber of which is sought in all the markets of the world—among the most important of which are the camphor wood, and those which produce gutta percha. The natives have for years been cultivating the sugar cane, cotton and tobacco, which grow to the greatest perfection. It produces all the spices known in commerce. The greater portion of the rataus which find their way to the United States, come from Borneo *via* Singapore, where the principal exports from the Island are shipped for Europe and the United States— about 500,000 bundles being exported annually. Ninetenths of all the antimony used in the world is brought from Borneo, where it exists in greater abundance and purity than in any other country. The export of this valuable metal from Singapore, all of which comes from Borneo, reaches from 3,000 to 5,000 tons annually.

It also produces large quantities of gold. The geological features of the Island are almost identical with those of the auriferous districts of Siberia, Australia, and California—consisting of lofty granite peaks, at the sides of which lay broad belts of schists, seyenites, and limestones, while at their base are broad placers, overlaying innumerable quartz veins. From these placers large quantities of gold are annually exported. This auriferous belt runs through the whole of the longest axis of the Island, extending from 1° south to 2° north. Of course, such a region is altogether unsuited for American or European miners to labor in, where labor is so cheap and abundant as it is in Borneo. There would be no necessity for white men to labor with their hands; but their capital and experience in such a field might be of immense advantage to the people of the Island, as well as to California.

The annual product of the Gold mines of Borneo, for several years past, has been between 350,000 and 400,000 ounces. Coal, of superior quality and most profuse abundance, exists, not alone in Borneo, but in several of the adjacent islands. The value of a supply of coal for the large fleet of war and commercial steamers constantly traversing the Chinese Sea induced the British Government, as far back as 1846, to purchase the Island of Labuan, where it has a splendid coal mine, which supplies its entire fleet; the coal, peculiarly well adapted for the purpose, being delivered on board the vessels at $1 25 per ton. It was through the influence of Mr. Brooke that the British Government obtained possession of this valuable Island. It is through the same gentleman's influence that American citizens have recently become possessed of several islands in the same group, which also contain extensive veins of equally good coal. It is impossible to overestimate the importance to American interests that a supply of coal in that vicinity may have in developing the rapidly increasing commerce between the United States and the Asiatic nations. If the recently inaugurated experiment of steam communication between San Francisco, China, and Japan shall be brought to a satisfactory result, and any considerable portion of the merchandise passing to and from those countries shall pass this way and over the great Pacific Railroad, the steamers which convey it must not be required to carry sufficient coal to serve for the entire passage of twenty-nine or thirty days, nor must commerce be taxed to pay for the cost of sending a supply of coal for their use at the enormous expense such an arrangement would necessarily involve. From this point of view the possession of a portion of Borneo, with its coal fields, is of paramount importance to American interests, not alone in that Island, but throughout Asia. Diamonds of great purity are found at several points on the main Island. These gems are so abundant that many of the Malays have several of great value set in their rings and uncouth jewelry. The Sultan of Matan, in 1850, obtained a Borneo diamond, which weighs 367 carats, and which has since been sold in

Europe for many thousand dollars. Iron ores of uncom-
mon purity, also exist in great profusion. To use the
words of a resident of the Island, when writing to a
friend, "I do not believe that in the same space there
can be found so great mineral and vegetable wealth in
the world."

. Its Facilities for Commerce.

The seacoast of Borneo exceeds 3,000 miles in extent.
Much of this coast is at present but little better than a
dense jungle; but most of this very vegetation, so dank
and tangled, and impeding to travel, has a commercial
value — the tough ratan, the worst of all these impedi-
ments, when cut down and tied in bundles, has a value in
Asia, Europe, and America. The interior of the Island
being exceedingly mountainous and well watered, innumerable rivers find a course to the sea, breaking the coast-
line into numerous channels for commerce to find its way
for hundreds of miles into the interior. The mouths of
twenty-three rivers on the southwest of the Island, all
navigable for upwards of one hundred miles, on an
average, for vessels drawing twelve feet of water, have
been examined by order of Rajah Brooke. Some of these
rivers have been navigated for upwards of two hundred
miles. The native merchants of Borneo own a number
of vessels, with which they carry the products of the
Island to Singapore for shipment to other portions of the
world. Most of these native vessels average about two
hundred tons burden, and in these they navigate the
rivers in all directions. The native trade, as far back as
1853, employed 25,000 tons of shipping. The exports for
the year exceeded $1,000,000 in value, and this export
trade has been more than trebled since. The section of
the Island granted to Rajah Brooke is intersected by two
navigable rivers, which greatly facilitate commerce.

Its People.—The Supply of Labor.

There are several races of people living on the Island of Borneo. The Malays, who came originally from the mainland, are the ascendent race, having subjugated the Dyaks—the aboriginal tribe. The fame of the Malay for intrepidity as a navigator, is only equaled by his notoriety as a pirate and freebooter. Centuries ago, when the ships that went to "far Ind" for spices, silks, and incense, were ill-constructed, slow, and poorly manned, these Malay pirates, who prowled over the trackless ocean as the Bedouin Arab prowls over the sandy deserts, met them hundreds of miles from the shore, and not unfrequently captured the trader, confiscated the cargo, and carried the crew into captivity. But the descendants of these pirates having been compelled to bow to the combined powers of steam, gunpowder, and necessity, have bent their energies to a better purpose, and now make remarkably fine sailors for the fleet of coasting craft, the lateen sails of which, seen in the distance, appear like specks of gold on the bright blue bosom of the broad ocean.

The Dyaks are a stout, muscular race, not much darker in complexion than the Chinese. They are tolerably good agriculturists, nearly all cultivating sugar cane, cotton, tobacco, etc. Many of them are also good mechanics and artificers in metal—Borneo sword blades being famous in India and Europe. The exhibition of the products and manufactures of the Borneoese at the World's Fair in London, in 1861, astonished all by their variety, beauty, and value. The superstitions of the Dyaks prevent them working in the mines, but the proximity of the Island to China has caused it to be well supplied with the cheap labor from that over populated country. These Chinese laborers are in one sense the most cosmopolitan of all races. Wherever bread is to be won, or gold amassed, there they go; thus becoming scattered all through southeastern

Asia and the adjoining islands. In one respect they are a great blessing to a country where labor is scarce. They are a laborious and thrifty race, of great benefit in the development of the resources of the country; but in some respects they are an element of great danger. They never identify themselves with the country in which they dwell; they simply strive to make all they can out of it, and carry it to their native land. They band themselves in secret organizations, and wield a powerful influence over the labor market in the East. It is this industrious class who perform all the labor in the mines at Borneo. The cost of their labor is a mere trifle compared to what their countrymen obtain in California. As many as ten may be hired for a less sum than a Chinese dishwasher receives in California. It is estimated that there are 500,000 Chinese on the Island at present—the total number of inhabitants exceeding 2,500,000.

The latest accounts represent the Island as exceedingly healthy and prosperous. The pirates, who but a few years back made the navigation of the Chinese Ocean extremely perilous, have been entirely destroyed or subjugated, and the coast of Borneo is now as safe from their depredations as the coast of California.

The Advantages it offers to California.

The possession of this extensive Island by a people desirous of cultivating feelings of friendship and close commercial relations with the United States, affords a rare opportunity to the merchants and enterprising adventurers who have gathered in California, seeking new fields for exploration. The same spirit which in but a few years has erected the frame work of a mighty empire on the Pacific coast, may do much towards giving the United States a station on the very threshhold of Asia, the door of which is now wide open, inviting our commerce and friendship.

A depot at which our war and merchant steamers, when in Asiatic waters, can obtain a supply of cheap and good coal, would be more valuable in furthering American interests in Asia then a hundred ministers plenipotentiary and consular agents. The establishment of an American company, or factory, as such companies are called in Asia, on an Island so rich in those rare spices, gums, perfumes, and woods as Borneo, is an era in national progress, and paves the way for the extension of not alone our commerce but our Republican institutions.

Under American superintendence, and by the aid of American skill and inventions, its gold and diamond mines will not long remain undeveloped. The wide extent of our country, with the varied nature of its soil and products of its many States, furnishes men who can enjoy vigorous health in any clime. The fear of the tropical heat, which has such an influence on the constitution of the sturdy Englishman, has no influence on the energetic young men raised in Florida, Louisiana, and Georgia, who have been accustomed from infancy to direct the work of an inferior race of laborers, under a burning sun, while cultivating sugar, cotton, and tobacco, all of which grow luxuriantly in Borneo.

It is certain that if the United States becomes a customer for the products of the Island, the two millions and a half of its inhabitants will purchase manufactured goods in return. Yankee thrift will not be long in proving to the keen Chinese laboring classes that American axes, pumps, and shovels are cheaper and better than any other; while sawing, planing, and other labor saving machines, will soon convince the intelligent Malays that the Americans are a people whose friendship is worth having.

The acquisition of a foothold at Borneo at this time, just when steam navigation has been inaugurated between San Francisco, China, and Japan, is most opportune, as furnishing convenient means of communication between the new acquisition and San Francisco. The spices and other products of Borneo will not be long in finding their way hither by these steamers, to be sent, fresh and fragrant, across the Isthmus or by the Pacific Railroad. Our local manufacturers may be greatly benefitted by this acquisition. There is nothing to prevent them making goods to suit the Borneo market, as the manufacturers of England do for the market of India. It is well known that most of the Asiatic ornaments and coins are made in England. The manufacturers of San Francisco, only yet in their infancy, will ere many years be active competitors with those of England in the Asiatic market—if not on the score of cheapness, certainly on that of the great superiority of their goods. The thousands of Chinese who have resided in San Francisco for years, and tested the merits of our home made goods and imbibed many of our "Yankee notions," will be agents for the introduction of our wares in their own country, without charging a commission for their services. Such of our readers as have watched the effect on the arts and manufactures of the civilized world by the utilization of India Rubber and Gutta Percha, which were scarcely known a quarter of a century ago, will not think us visionary when we state that it is highly probable that all the valuable vegetable products of such a partially explored Island as Borneo have not yet been discovered. Who is better adapted for finding them out than the keen, educated American citizen, who, taught in our public schools, has sufficient knowledge of botany and chemistry to detect new substances and to test their value. There is one fact connected with the Island of Borneo we had almost forgotten to mention. Unlike all other tropical Islands, no venomous reptiles or insects or ferocious animals exist on it. No such thing as a poisonous snake or animal dangerous to man has been seen on the Island.

With reference to the importance of the United States possessing a foothold in Borneo, it may be proper to state that when England purchased the Island of Labuan it was asserted by English statesmen that its acquisition went far to make England mistress of the Chinese Sea. Borneo is infinitely better adapted for commerce and settlement than Labuan. It lies in the center between the two most important ports in that sea—Hongkong on the north and Singapore on the south. Its being under the influence of American interests may therefore deprive our great maritime rival of some of her boasted supremacy in that quarter of the globe.

Hoping that this hurriedly written pamphlet will prove sufficiently interesting to direct further inquiry to the subject, which we hope may lead to a practical attempt to extend American commerce in Borneo, the author respectfully submits it to the careful consideration of the reader.

PREFACE TO ADDENDA.

Being confident that the intuitive love of liberty, inherent in all mankind, is not alone propagated by the daily advance in knowledge through the regular channels of education, infallibly ordained to lift high up to the surface of civilization all of God's most glorious images on earth—but that it is the imperative duty of all those having reached said surface, while there they commence their perigrinations through life hand in hand with none but brethren in intensest love and chilklike faith in God the Father, to draw after them the vast remainder of mankind high up to the same evergreen surface of the most happy terrestrial life allotted to each on earth, hopeful for eternity.

That we, the American Nation, having this year set foot in Asia, the vastest division of the globe, by far the most densely peopled, millions and millions of whom are steeped in ignorance, are going there to commence our brotherly labor of educating the millions, hand in hand with our commercial interests.

That we will make subservient to civilization the amassed labor of these millions, and attain a greatness as a nation of the free, which all other methods of non-republican governments have failed to reach. I hold firm to the most undeniable fact, that we have arrived at a power, both moral and physical, among all the nations of the earth, and as it took us but 91 years, with 35,000,000, to achieve this end, while the united remainder of the civilized world — write the year 1867 after Christ, that our educatory system is the grand secret of it—the most colossal pedestal of liberty.

That we, as well as Europe and all the rest of civilized mankind, barely comprise one-quarter of the living beings, it becomes, upon the above facts, conclusive, that in centuries to come the remaining three-quarters of mankind, when civilized, will testify to our method of political fellowship and educatory system for all good and beneficial purposes combined, being the one which carried it and was inaugurated in the year 1776, Christian Era, by the American Nation.

As to commerce most immediately, it has always been a happy contemplation of mine to fancy united mankind, when civilized, to figure in the lists of supply and demand, additional to what the mother earth yields to husbandry. That the figures will be written with unpronounceable noughts, in proportion to the wants of the civilized man against the poverty of the barbarian, is our inheritance to-day, in after ages, thousands of years to come.

To the most conspicuous advocate of education living, to a gentleman from whose hands I myself received letters of introduction, many years ago in London, to Mr. George Peabody, are humbly dedicated these grateful lines.

WM. E. F. KRAUSE.

San Francisco, Cal., July 4th, 1867.

2

APPENDIX.

The startling intelligence which came over the wires on the 6th of February and 5th of July to the *Bulletin*, and on the 12th of March to the *Alta California*, of a wealthy trading Company having, in Boston and New York, organized and already bought the northern part of one of the richest islands in the world—Borneo—has been hailed by California with immense joy.

For not only do we see in this first and firm foothold outside of our vast continent, a future State of the U. S., exactly on the principle on which the Honorable East India Company was founded by Lord Clyde, which increased so fabulously in wealth as to virtually encroach upon the prerogative of the crown, and to be elevated to a Vice Royalty of the British Empire as a matter of political necessity—but we suddenly see ourselves enabled to plant and harvest our own spices, and to emancipate ourselves from the, commercially, very humiliating thraldom of being considered by Asiatics a very rich, first-class cash customer, unable to work himself from want of chance; not possessing, in spite of our power, any territory there of our own. Therefore, with this acquisition of a vast extent of territory within the tropics, bought without bloodshed, and paid for in hard cash, we are now a commercial whole. We have thus suddenly gained the products of virtually 30 latitudes, by settling de facto upon 7, 6, 5 Northern Hemisphere, and on land of our own, where our increasing shipping, both commercial and naval vessels, go without soliciting the hospi-

tality of the English at Hongkong, and others in Asia
generally.

The rush to this youngest born territory of the United
States, from Boston, New York, New Orleans, and San
Francisco, will reach vast dimensions, upon the natural
fondness of the old for the young, upon the propensity of
the American to explore and to venture, and upon the
strength of his mind over the more physical man.

To fully enumerate the advantages which the United
States at large will derive from this territory in a commercial, a political, and especially in a social point of view, will
soon be the province of a host of novelists. Suffice for us
here to state, that the productions of Borneo are very rich
and manifold. Of vegetable productions, as before stated,
pepper is produced, the nutmeg and cloves indigenous and
peculiar, besides rice, coffee, sugar, indigo, tobacco, and
all such other valuable products as are usual in tropical
countries.

For ages Borneo has been known to be rich in diamonds
and gold, and as to climate, it is far more healthful than is
generally the case near the equator, owing to the genial
influence of the sea breezes. The aborigines, who occupy
the interior, are Papuans; very warlike, but who will soon
yield to the pacific persuasions of our missionaries. In the
mean time, our many naval armaments and forces constantly near or in sight of the main settlements, will look to their
protection against Malays, until we are sufficient in number
to meet emergencies of that sort. In a social point of view
the settlement will, at first, form an aspect similar to our
California in '49—a heterogenous concourse of the most
intelligent and enterprising of the human family at large.

What applied to the San Francisco of California in '49,
is applicable to the San Francisco of Borneo in '67, so that
we are sure of seeing there scenes re-enacted which form
here now the annals of our beloved Eureka. Our naval
stations will no doubt form the pride of the settlement and

of the nation, and of piracies little will be heard of in future by all our merchants.

The settlement being due south from Hongkong, can be reached within three days from there, making a total of four weeks from San Francisco by steamer. Twenty-six days we go to Hongkong among strangers, three days more and we are at home. As if the vast Pacific were a pond, we bridge it now in a month and land among 600,000,000 of intelligent beings. In immediate proximity are three civilized nations—the English, Dutch, and Spanish, so that the commercial houses, which will at once be started by our San Francisco, New York, and Boston merchants, have a vast field opened to them in their reciprocated trade with Singapore, Batavia, and Manila, the export of flour from here being the first staple in the grand list of supplies. From Borneo we will sell it to north—Manila, the Spanish; south—Singapore, the English; and further south—Batavia, the Dutch; within a few days delivery from Borneo.

Exactly this section of Borneo is most judicious indeed, and immense must be the reward of those who will be the Pioneers of Borneo. Almost all products of Borneo, and the small islands adjacent, form the lightest kind of freight for the Colorado and other steamers of our new China Mail line, at once affording to the new territory advantages which many old settled commercial communities do not possess, viz: those of finding a speedy, ready, and profitable market in the United States, everywhere.

Our Boston and New York Clipper Ships for San Francisco will increase in proportion to the export trade of pepper, coffee, and dyewoods from Borneo, the usual charters remaining for loading Teas *via* Cape of Good Hope, until our Pacific Railroad is finished, by 1869, with which will cease these time-costing circumnavigations of the globe *via* both capes.

A superior advantage the new settlement will have from the beginning, in finding the native Malay race a very intelligent one, and being rather dense, our San Francisco and Eastern Manufacturers, by a lively interest taken at the start, secure to themselves an additional consumer of all such home-made goods as are indispensible to mankind generally, and desired by the young territory in particular.

In return we may expect to be kept in constant excitement by every steamer and vessel arriving, bringing to our shores productions besides the regular articles of commerce indigenous to Malaysia, which are different species, hitherto unknown for the simple reason that the white race were, throughout the East Indian Archipelago, too few in number to bring to light, far less to exhaust those priceless treasures.

The scientific world with us on the Occident, the Smithsonian Institute at the head of it, the directors of the botanical and the zoological gardens in all the leading cities of the Union to follow, will be on tiptoe all the while by the receipt of rare botanical species—of birds of paradise —of all kinds of mammalia of the highest order, ourang-outangs, elephants, etc.   The Sooloo Islands, close by, are again rich in pearls; in short, an endless interest is attached to our new tropical territory.

What more superior allegory can here be found than that the Tree of Liberty, planted in '76, throws this day its tallest branch over to a small spot in the Orient and shelters it.   For the American is this day called upon to enter into a new and busy scene of his masterly activity—to approach the dense population of Malaysia, not with sword and scepter in hand, nor with violence, as tit for tat, but with the powerful manly love for the stranger, whom to take by his brotherly hand and to draw him forth from his dark hut and to bring him to light, soul and body together, will be his method for attaining to the most brilliant results in every conceivable point of view.   Such a proceeding will contain the grand nucleus of sure success, viz: while we commence operations on his mind by educating him forthwith in free schools on the spot, he will, intelligent as he de facto is, emerge from his nudity of body first and foremost, which makes him at once a consumer in a commercial point of view of our suitable Lowell and San Francisco manufactures of cotton and wool fabrics, increasing in proportion to his advance in general civilization. This system of feeding the mind of the Papuan and the Malay with a novel and light food, instead of the old feudal course of subduing and muddling the head with noxious drugs and poisonous fire-waters, will bring about all the advantages to commerce which a dense civilized community offers as consumers of merchandise, and of course very speedily. While it took the Spaniards, Portugese, Dutch, and even the English, complete ages to coerce into submissiveness such vast millions, and to draw forth the reputed wealth—for which purpose thei: colonies exist—we may attain to the same end in comparatively a brief space of time.

Upon the platform of universal education have we here attained our strength, in not alone a commercial, but a political point of view, and we plant these principles this day in Borneo. The civilized Malay in time—civilized as per education only—has, like any other educated person, the love of liberty and of labor within himself as a dowry from Heaven. As with the education of any man rises the Phœnix of self governing himself, so will, in an incredibly short lapse of time, cease the violent outburst of passion and give way to traits of self-denial and brotherly affection. Their sultans will cease to exist the moment the people equal them in knowledge, without any other interference on our part than of educating them. The great difficulty of finding willing labor under the vertical rays of a tropical sun is thus overcome. The paradisiacal country itself, surrounded by the most charming spots on the face of the globe, will therefore be a fit abode for Americans. Where love rules, there is happiness—there is wealth and greatness.

Near the coast of Borneo are Sarawak and Labuan, colonies of England, well governed by the brave Sir James

Brooke, so that we have everywhere surrounding us the most interesting neighborhood. The great rice producing island of Celebes is but a short distance southeast of us, while we almost touch on our way from Hongkong the well known Manila of the Philipine Islands. To the immediate west is the rising free port Singapore. Further southwest the celebrated Batavia, all of whom being Europeans, owning said countries and living there, will take our flour which they cannot get from anywhere nearer. No tropics producing cereals, we thus find a new and strictly additional permanent customer for our California flour, an item of such vast importance that it must secure to every farmer the best and firmest prices for his superabundant crops in all future, simply because we have become their nearest neighbors producing this most necessary staff of life, to all Europeans and others.

THE NEW AMERICAN SETTLEMENT IN BORNEO IN A COSMOPOLITAN POINT OF VIEW.

The vast commerce of the United States, attained in 91 years, has now spread to another division of the globe. With this memorable year begins a new era of its progress, which embodies in its future development the exhaustion of the indigenous resources of the Asiatic tropics. We have now an almost uninterrupted soil of our own, down to the spice regions of the equator. We have gained most important latitudes. Untold millions will henceforth be saved to the country of the innumerable products of the tropics, which other nations supplied us with; and as these products cover many of the most indispensible ones to our necessities, and are second to none except the wheat in commercial importance, we may well predict to our future home within the tropics that advantage to the United States and its commercial interests which must necessarily crown with the most brilliant success the intelligent and far seeing founders of it.

The fact of the existence of such fabulous products in the tropics of Asia, and the necessity of using them and of producing them having for ages past brought the nations of Europe there in rotation of power—Europe ceasing at 36 north as we do 30 north—we now likewise appear on the spot to develop its resources. With the peculiar method of our own to achieve success, as illustrated by our greatness this very day among the nations of the earth, we shall forthwith set to work to assimilate the natives of our new home to our own standard of civilization by educating them in public free schools among us there. While by so operating we not alone perform a charitable task, simply doing what we do at home, but we make them at once subservient to our interests, through them and their suitable labor to make the settlement thrive to mutual advantage.

The coercive measures of the European nations have not alone politically and socially, but commercially, tended to frustrate their best interests, inasmuch as with the elevation, instead of the subjugation of each native, there must be a demand created for the attributes of civilization which our manufactures supply and our commerce supports. If we now take into consideration that our new home, with its neighboring Islands, has the dense native population of two and a half millions, we may at once calculate upon in time supplying them with prints, muslins, calicos, etc., from Lowell, San Francisco and other cities of our Union, thus creating an entirely new and vast demand, which immediately and directly benefits ourselves.

As the Malay race is well known to be intelligent, our mode of friendly intercourse with men, so natural to us who know no restraint and are so brotherly linked together in our home of liberty and freedom, will at once make them confiding and win their hearts, curious and true and dormant in all mankind; so that what all other nations can never achieve by force among Asiatics, and have therefore as yet not accomplished, although ages have passed, we will arrive at in comparatively a short time, viz : of civilizing them by lifting them up, in our public schools and friendly intercourse with them, to the surface of our own political and social plateau, which knows no other altitude but that of intellectual and moral greatness. We thus secure them as customers and consumers of our home-made manufactures, besides their labor in the field, on the plantation, in the mines and at sea. All these advantages will again compound, as the grains of wheat on a chess-board, into such a chaos at last that we are bound to make giant strides in our own national interest. As the observances of a savage are very acute, and there exists a complete affinity between the natives of the entire East Indian Archipelago, in the same manner as the numerous clusters of the picturesque isles forming Malaysia received their paradisiacal verdure through zephyrs wafting the seeds from one to another, so they will communicate their happiness to others, and we augment in peace and comfort to ourselves what has been the vain effort of every other nation. We will thus involuntarily draw a constantly increasing demand for our manufactures, be sure of the most efficient labor at all times, and perhaps never be called upon to display our formidable strength towards any of them. As upon psychological grounds was written the Declaration of Independence, as the Star of Liberty forever shines and illuminates the hearts and the souls of all mankind, so it is only a matter of time that its light reaches the remaining divisions of the globe.

The philanthropist—the true American—therefore, will most solemnly treat this subject, while stepping upon the soil of another division of the globe. With the religious task of grafting the tree of Liberty amidst the dense barbarous millions of Asia, a new era of his own individual social and political superiority commences, gently and constantly expanding the periphery of his influence for the benefit of civilization of the world at large and his own national gratification in particular. With the stupendous power which the soul wields over the body, will the yearning millions embrace Christianity, will bless this country of the free, and love its citizens as common brethren of one father. They will thus commence to rise and awaken from the lethargic stupor of their previous existence, and soon present to us and the world at large the interesting aspect of great naivete at first, until, as in true accordance with all nature, the amalgamating power of good from evil will make conspicuous men who may be the pride of the world.

I draw my reflection from the fact that in a circumnavigation of the globe from here in 1855, the tropics of Asia everywhere, and Malaysia especially, presented to me such loveliness of scenery, in their islands and peninsulas, that the gift of man adequately to express his delight at beholding it, is paralyzed. If thus God placed the Malay within the tropics of Asia, on spots so elysian, is it not a finger-sign of His that the intellect of His children there is commensurate of appreciating it? Does not the vivacity of the native prove at once the existence, force, and power of that same intellect, which all mankind is endowed with, from the forlorn inhabitant of Enderby's Island to the diminutive Esquimaux of Greenland?

To draw forth this natural gift is the object of Christianity—to diffuse it, the object of our free public schools among them—to make it available for good to themselves and the world at large, the object of appropriate and voluntary labor, which we go there to direct for the benefit of our commerce, and to recompense to them in full with our blessings of intellectuality, of political fraternity, and of national liberty.

Wherever American citizens settle they carry the inalienable rights of free men with them; for, inasmuch as every citizen by his vote becomes part of the Government, so is the United States Government ever ready to protect him and his home.

We therefore find ourselves within the jurisdiction of the United States on this grant of land in northern Borneo, legitimately our own by purchase of responsible owners, and the native inhabitants of the interior, the Papuans, originally occupying a similar position to our Apaches, while the Malay of the coast is often as intelligent as the Cherokee. Their numbers are millions. To attempt to even conceive, far less possibly to arrange in figures, the multitudinous commercial advantages accruing from an, henceforth, enlightened community, demanding supplies of our home-made manufactures, altogether additional and new in our columns of supplies, would be more than vain indeed. If we add thereto the unfailing effect of a grateful voluntary labor, permanent to us as is the light of knowledge which we this day take to their shores and plant within them, on our cultivation of the land there we may not alone be sure of the most happy result in all respects, but establish the truism of our glorious institutions there.

In comparison, as it took the nations of Europe literally thousands of years, by their autocratic sway, to arrive at religious, political, and commercial ends of to-day, it has taken us, so far, 91 years to stand on a par in power with the most powerful of them. And how can it be otherwise? We lift, every day, every one domiciled with us to the surface of knowledge by our schools; while there, since time immemorial, far over 200,000,000, out of 280,000,000, can neither read nor write. Forever lost to commerce have therefore been the lives of millions since thousands of years. All their literary knowledge—the knowledge of a few—never reached the darkness of the millions, and how can it penetrate in a system of chasms of society, one more slippery than the other, down, deep down to the slum of abject poverty, the vast and worm-eaten pedestal of their history.

The glorious sun, the element of life, of everything created, when he shines forth his rays touch God's entire creation. We have copied from this work of God; as he animates the tiniest violet as well as man, as the sun never sets without its admonishing nature to rest, our glorious institutions, which make all men equal before the law, and indispensible to one another, and which draw a phalanx around us 35,000,000 this day which is of divine — — strength. We thus find ourselves of equal strength in general civilization with the rest of the world. What must henceforth be the hight of civilization when decenium after decenium, century after century, the world's 1,000,000,000 will be enlightened? Mankind will be one brotherhood in love and faith to God. That era dates from 1776; 1867 carries the joyful truth to Asia.

The plateau life of the people of the United States against the terrace architecture of the rest of the world, when viewed by birds-eye, presents the sun of liberty warming all of us, while all others but partially receive its animating rays.

As the mother earth gives the germinating power to nature, without which the brightest rays of the sun are but accessory, so is education—the necessity of man to learn that he is a man—the proudest acknowledgment of his to God! The mother of liberty! Wherever we tread we educate; each Asiatic must learn to point his finger to the east—the Capitol of Washington. The large occident is not large enough to draw hither the remainder of mankind from the remaining divisions of the created globe, therefore, true to nature, we must go to them. As their bodies, which contain their souls, cannot all come to us, we must go to their bodies and there nourish their souls. The divine rights of nature are always and everywhere true. The city of Washington is this day but small in comparison with New York and other cities of the Union, so is it with Christ's birthplace—almost forsaken.

Besides, plants best thrive when left undisturbed. Science propogates. No doubt a fact that as the vast continent of America was but thinly inhabited by Indians when first discovered, it is according to nature that Europeans of the Teutonic, the Celtic, the Gallic, and the Anglo Saxon descendants acclimate themselves well here. That here should be the cradle of liberty is equally true to nature; the quiet of the American forest developing its most prodigious trees.

So became the tree of liberty indigenous to America. All the nations of the universe cannot disturb it. Their shots at forts now would but singe a few leaves, as much as any civil war is but a stray mole, the teeth of which soon break at the hardness of the tiniest root of it.

Imbued with the godliness of liberty, the very reflection that a non-appreciation by others has often to be deplored, points to education; for as the wealthiest among the Asiatic Sultans and Rajahs are now and then the most ignorant or intolerant, or both, it proves that their power is evanescent, and that nations whose millions wander blindfolded, are but automatons when encountered by men who carry the flag of independance.

Thus the few who among the millions of the earth wander hand in hand under the broad canopy of enlightenment can never awaken sympathy in the autocrat, and to believe that any non-republican nation in Europe, Asia, or anywhere, can politically sympathise with us at any time, must make such mind border on idiosyncrasy. The moment the swimmer's head rises above the surface of the water, he breathes, he lives, he gains strength, his mind comprehends, hope animates his soul, he feels God and salvation to shield him farther; so are we, the few. I speak of, the 35,000,000 out of 1000. We have risen to the surface and are free and safe to reach the shores of heavenly eternity, after the sublunary trial of labor, of unselfishness and of faith in the so pointedly veiled and interestingly hopeful future.

Upon this fact rests history, that in the sea of intellectual darkness for thousands of years the millions of God's children were steeped and kept by violence below the surface by a few despots, comparatively speaking, and although God sent his Son to prevent their ever perishing, yet but 35,000,000, and a trifle more, in this memorable year of 1867 after Christ, have reached the surface of the water, to live in the christian hope that some future age will hail freedom to all. I say 35,000,000, so much to say, that I give no credit to isolated individuals, who in other countries exert themselves to aid their brethren.

There exists no excuse in crammed millions too dense to be reached with A B C books, with kindness and with goodness. The purple and Washington, immoral weakness and moral strength, the impenetrable deep and the calm surface of hope and safety. I said before, we 35,000,000 can now, after 91 years, defy the world of 965,000,000, after a lapse of 1867 years. What will our power be henceforth? additional love, brotherly assistance, sympathy, and all the indirect means which will reach them, to gain the courage of men.

It is not an easy undertaking to enlighten millions, as my figures have thus shown, and to see all monarchies totter and Pagans made Christians, is easier said than done. There is the difference in the capacity of minds for education, so immense that even with us we have encountered ingratitude, incapacity and darkness of mind, which is fully on a par with those of the nude and forlorn capacities of other nations. For those our pity, our schools, and stern precautions against reoccurrences of the sort, or else by a blind revenge instead of a national forgiveness properly timed, we are no better than the autocrat of a monarchy, who fears the approach of his millions to the surface. The hydra of stubbornness and passion with us can no more be feared to lap at the vitals of our tree of liberty, planted to shelter all creation, than the indigenous grizzly of our beloved California could run against Daniel Webster in the Calaveras grove of trees and make it shake; he will most assuredly dash out his brains, and hold in his paws some of its moss perhaps. The bear species is also in Europe, but not so the soil of America. We might send for curiosity's sake some of it to Professor Ehrenberg for micro-. scopical examination; how many organic and inorganic forms he can bring to light, whether they are phytolitharia and bacillariæ, or polythalamia or arcellina—in short, whether the fumarole of our few ignorami is quiescent.

As on terra firma, an abundant earth, forming invisibly powerful organic life is constantly going on, so do the minds of the free, every day, elucidate their active, minute life, while deriving their substance from observation of God's infallible, endless works of nature.

The great canopy of heaven with its countless stars leads us to regard the sun as God's most impressive work, because we are taught to inhabit but a planet of minor magnitude, and therefore placed at the extreme opposite of whatever stars we behold. Thus we arrive at the contemplation of space; and when we acknowledge to ourselves that we loose our grasp at comprehending the vastness of the universe, the distance, for instance, between us and Venus, we meekly return to our given sphere of faith, hope, and charity. What being is forsaken under the canopy of heaven with a soul within him that is clear as the azure blue of willful sin! What wealth and greatness on earth more gratifying and exalted than a spotless name, and President of the United States, and men of progress.

I shall now give a synopsis of the important geographical location of our settlement at Borneo, as a center within a close circle of European colonies, from which to diffuse our shipments of flour, etc., to them, permanently and additionally to what our exports from San Francisco are this day.

The Sunda Islands constitute: 1. Sumatra, with Banka, and the groups of Nicobar, Andaman, and the Cocos. 2. Java, with Madura, Bali, Lombok, Sumbawa, the Postilions, and Paternosters, Sandalwood, Flores, and Timor. 3. The Bandas and the Moluccas. 4. Celebes, and the small islands adjacent. 5. The Philipine and Bashee groups. Borneo lies between latitude 4° 13′ south, and 7° 5′ northern hemisphere, so as to be almost evenly divided by the equator, and between longitude 108° 52′ and 119° 20′ east. From north to southwest, the island

is washed by the Chinese Sea; on the south, it faces the
Sea of Java; on the east, it is separated by the Strait of
Macassar from Celebes; and northward, for 250 miles, its
shores are washed by the Sea of Celebes. Here also, on
the northeastern side, are the celebrated Sooloo Islands,
which are very rich in pearls.

Borneo is well watered within—lakes and lagoons are
numerous. The largest river is the Brunai; the other
large rivers are the Rejang, Sarebus, the Batang, Loopar,
the Sarawak, Sambas, and Kapooas. The deltas at the
mouths of these rivers overflow, making the soil extremely
fertile. The forests of Borneo are very dense.

A chain of lofty mountains stretches from the northeast
to southwest, with the Kinibaloo as the highest peak, in
latitude 6° 8′ and longitude 116° 33′. Its elevation above
the level of the sea is 13,680 feet. Near this mountain is
the largest lake of Borneo, bearing the same name as the
highest mountain—Kinibaloo.

To form an idea of the wealth to be derived from our
new settlement, that the resources are the vastest and
richest imaginable, suffice it to say, that the neighboring
Dutch estimate their annual crop of nutmegs at 1,000,000lbs;
of mace at 250,000lbs; and of cloves at 500,000lbs.

The clove is the flower-bud of an evergreen myrtle. The
nutmeg tree has some resemblance to the pear, the fruit is
of the size and form of an apricot; as it ripens, the outer
coating falls off and displays the nut covered with the
beautiful red reticulation called "mace."

The immense advantage of abundant labor on the spot,
by a race of people both intelligent and hardy, and whose
home has been on these islands for ages, cannot but make
curious the most eager economist. We, going there, to at
once finding such labor, the most efficient and consummate
by a proper, kind approach to them, by a study how to at
once ameliorate their sufferings, incidental to barbarism
and polytheism, we at once will gain what other nations
thought injudicious—their confidence. True to our stan-
3

dard of civilization, we shall beget confidence by our frank
behaviour and natural kindness to them, attending to their
wants, while we develop the country and pursue our commerce. We will here gain without an effort what other
nations never attain. As the fruit of three breadfruit trees
will support a native for a year, and as the country con-
tains endless forests of such and similar indigenous vegeta-
tions, a Californian might forever calculate to estimate the
expense of labor on a plantation up to the time when education will make the Malay rise to demand his due. He
must have new rubrics for bits and cents, and fractions in
his ledgers, and extra wideness for the column of dollars
on the credit side of returns.

What Asiatic labor is capable of at their homes, one has
simply to take any book of history at hand and refer to a
description of the world-renowned Chinese Wall, which is
over one thousand miles long, and is nearly as perfect to-
day as when it was built two thousand years ago.

But not in this light only do we see our own direct advantages, that by a friendly approach and naturally urbane
treatment we best lead them to perform their labor—but we
will see the time come when our mutually friendly intercourse and familiarity, as the reward for labor best performed,
will make these millions appear in our markets for all sorts
of supplies, in imitation of our own requirements. It is
to this vastness of demand that we owe now our maritime
greatness. What will it be when 2,500,000 Malays, of a
division of the globe containing 600,000,000, arrive in the
columns of our commercial schedules? Can the mind
fathom what commerce will have to supply when one thousand millions of the earth's inhabitants demand the com-
forts of civilization, and that all the united boasted civilization of this day but clads bearly the half of mankind after
a lapse of thousands of years?

THE TROPICS OF THE UNITED STATES.

It is utterly impossible to adequately estimate the importance of the step taken by our merchants in the China and India trade to secure a vast tract of land within the tropics, including the very region of the equator, where spices grow only. I allude to the northern portion of the great Island of Borneo, in Malaysia, which has been so patriotically thus acquired. Without bloodshed this has been done—an aid to our Government, which is so unexpected as it is effectual, to lessen the awful burden which oppresses it so much at this very moment, by keeping all possible foreign invoice amounts in the country to assist it in paying the war debt.

To make the heart of every American pulsate at this enormous scheme, let it be known that over $10,000,000,000 this country must have paid to the Dutch and Chinese for spices, dyewoods, drugs, coffee, tea, etc., during the last ninety-one years. In order to realize in some measure these figures, fancy yourself every family from Maine to Texas, from Washington Territory to Florida, using at every meal at least half a dozen of substances derived from Asiatic tropics, without any reciprocation profitable to our industry. When your mind is thus awed—when you emerge from the stupor to reflect upon the waste of money perpetrated during nearly a century—then you will somewhat comprehend how truly gigantic is the advantage gained from this year onward to the people and the country by the above acquisition, and furthermore how *apropos* come these invoice amounts, henceforth saved to the people so unavoidably taxed to sustain in action the Union which they love and cherish. What incalculably beneficial effect must such assistance beget in every point of view. Words are inadequate ; history only carries one out of this dilemma—how every European nation of political rank went there to enrich itself. Just like Europe, so have we no tropical country of our own; we cease at 30, they at 36. We must therefore go to Asia likewise, to secure such islands on the equator of Asia, where the spices grow only, as are this day in savage hands. We have but to cross from San Francisco in two months by vessel; they have, from Europe, to double the Cape of Good Hope in four months to get there. As the Europeans require five weeks *via* Suez, and we but four weeks by the China Mail Line from San Francisco, we have an advantage over Europe by steam likewise in the development of territories in tropical Asia. Besides, there are innumerable islands due southeast, which contain equally fabulous wealth, having no legitimate owners, and all in the way of our commerce from New York to San Francisco. Their spices will proceed here like the tea from China, to be sent by railroad to New York—the vessels loading wheat for Liverpool.

The enterprise in question is especially timely, and no doubt suggested by the founders of the China Steam Line, whose object must be to avoid tresspassing on the hospitality of any nation permanently.

The future American city of Palaces, in Malaysia, reached in three days from the present terminus at Hongkong, with its grand staple, the diamond, will no doubt rival any city of the Orient in splendor, because distance lends enchantment, and all Americans will feel interested in its growth and contribute to its immediate magnificence.

We have now arrived at a strength, both moral and political, equal to any nation on earth; we can therefore acquire in peace all unclaimed Oceanica—a mere pastime for our nation to hold, in comparison to the gain of a million a day henceforth for ages.

One of the most conspicuous advantages derived from the above acquisition is the native labor, which, unlike the African and Chinese with us, is there indigenous, therefore more natural, willing, and effective at the outset, besides plentiful.

As a great civilized nation we go there and to them;

kind and comforting instead of despotically maltreating
and stupefying them, thus gaining another advantage of
such magnitude as only to be comprehended partially, by
our progress and power during 91 years, to have equaled
civilized Europe in 1867 years.

I allude to our plateau life against the European terrace
architecture, which latter kept the native of Asia, on soil
possessed by a power in Europe, in such nudity of body
and general poverty, as to have lost him forever as a customer for their manufactures, which supplies their ships
would have carried; all of which is *vice versa* with us. We lift
him gradually up to the light of comprehending that he is
in this world to labor, to eat his bread cheerfully, and that
he can take to labor as a fancy, and can become great in,
and respected by it.

To judge from the Chinese, the Malay is similarly endowed, therefore immense progress in civilization can be
gained, as they are unpolluted by concentrated paganism,
while the large, united, and complete Chinese nation have,
as votaries of Confucius, for ages past been found difficult
of access to embrace Christianity.

The purchase of the land being ere this completed, and
the President of the New York Chamber of Commerce
having passed through here, and on the 1st of January, 1867,
sailed per " Colorado," to China, has no doubt gone there
and settled all preliminaries on the spot, so that it is no
further an indiscretion to call all America up to attention.
The price, it is supposed, having been got at as cheaply as
possible, and having paid the money as well as all docu-
ments receipted, San Francisco may hail this day. Untold
millions will enter her harbor at once, for nearly all spices
form steamer freight, and our steam communication is permanent, and assisted by subsidies from the Government to
carry the mails.

I return to the commercial vastness of the question.
Next to flour, we daily consume more tropical productions
than any thing else. Our land ceases at the Gulf of Mexi-

co. We cannot extend south, because we meet with young
republics. We are not an aggressive nation, and therefore
do not covet our greatness at the expense of the happiness
of the only republican-brethren we have got.   We rather
assist them in their growth of republics—as much as the
Monroe Doctrine is a household word, an everlasting bar-
rier against Europe.

We therefore go to Malaysia, where we do not trespass,
but do good. We eat the spices, we cannot do without
them, we therefore must have them. We are equally intelligent to produce them, as any other nation on earth;
even tea we may arrive at in Malaysia, the privilege of the
Chinese and Japanese, in China and Japan, at present. We
will save to the commerce of the United States, invoice
amounts, which otherwise would continue to enrich the
Dutch, Chinese, and others, large enough in amount to
create a glow of excitement and of wonder throughout the
Union.   What a noble satisfaction for our future tropical
sister States, to be ahead of all other States, except perhaps
our beloved California, in the assistance to the debt-ridden
and oppressed Government to liquidate its liabilities.

Holding firm and unabated to the fact that we daily consume in amount more spices, coffee, and tea than anything
else, except flour, we were never as yet a complete commercial country, and we of course never should be, were
we not to secure such lands on the equator where the pepper is indigenous, the nutmeg, clove, cinnamon, coffee,
and the drugs indispensible to us and civilization.   That
all the States of the present Union form but the half of
what the Union will and must be when we ourselves plant
within our own jurisdiction whatever we consume and
therefore need.   Every article we import shows a want of
progress not to have it ourselves; it proves that we are less
eager and pushing than those who furnish us with the
same. As to excuses that we cannot compete in certain
manufactures, because the down-trodden millions abroad
enable the foreigner to compete with us, against tariff and

charges, they are founded on the fact of carelessness, that
we, being rich, prefer the convenience of not stirring to do
it ourselves, but furthermore, allow our copper ores, cotton, etc., to go abroad, to come back to us in kettles and
stockings, and to pay the Dutch money for their pepper.

Already Franklin wore a homespun coat; why should
we forget his wisdom while we revere his memory? Un-
less we commence as well as we can, we can never finish
brilliantly. Why be timid? Europe has this day a very
questionable advantage over us, which consists in a greater
multitude. Their labor is cheap—the offspring of despotism.
Europe was mainly peopled from Asia, and we from Europe; therefore we continue to absorb exactly the talent
which there is so poorly and inadequately recompensed.
Added to which, our crude resources to an inexhaustible
extent, we come to the point that we need nothing from
Europe but the living man. In him we draw hither the
very art to make those superior qualities of goods which
commerce and civilization demand—therefore additional
talent, usefulness, and vigor; while we hold out to him the
hand of fellowship and lead him to the post where he is best
fitted to shine among us, according to the degree of his
intellect and will to labor.

Each emigrant from Europe loosens the pedestal on
which there stands the throne. Half Europe in America,
and not a vestige of any throne remains.

To influence said artisans by hundreds to immigrate and
permanently settle with us, the millionaires must be ap-
pealed to. The born American, if millionaire in years
after—the man of character and of goodness of heart, always accessible and courteous to the stranger, and ready
for a few minutes to listen to business ideas; as manufac-
turer, paying his workmen liberally; as landlord, not hard;
as capitalist, foremost in sagacity not to loose his millions,
the toil of years; as a citizen, cherishing within him the
inextinguishable love for the imperishable Union—the land
of Freedom for the world. Such a millionaire, all over the

United States, is always easily persuaded to invest in national enterprises, incompatible otherwise to a mind so astute and clear that it eschews at all times the very idea of viewing money in any other light than to be there as the assistant by which to carry out his intellectual ideas. His family and relatives comfortably provided for, he will indulge, like Mr. Peabody, in the exquisite gratification of distributing nationally his millions before he dies, that they bear additional fruit on the Tree of Liberty, which sheltered him in life, and enabled him to expand to such prodigious growth of worldly success. It is this identical American, God bless him, who will send the ships to Europe and invite the emigrant on board free of any charge.

The foreign born, if millionaire, in years after, and naturalized, is not so easily induced to enter into enterprises which admit the scrutiny of the people. His habits are the main cause of his reluctance. These do not conform to the off-hand, friendly, social intercourse with everybody. Sometimes vanity, pomp, and pride adhere to him here—the offsprings of the European system of social abeyance—and impede more high-minded actions on his part. It is hard for him to die; he hopes to sleep sounder in the costly catacomb, as he has lived in palaces seen in Paris, and preferred them to the quiet Park of Ashland, with its well read library.

The foreign millionaire at last, who alights at the club and at once wishes himself back to Europe, yet never leaves, takes no interest whatever in our national enterprises. On the contrary, he is apt to sneer at the country, the institutions, the Government, especially the Customhouse and taxation—pooh-poohing everything. His life is of no benefit to society, either private or public; his face is not seen in the drawing-rooms of his associates in wealth; he sits too long over the dessert of his dinner at the club, to be at all excusable, *d'apres le stricte menu du Baron de Brisse.* In public he is unsocial to all republicans, from his European habits and prejudices.

The very sight of a man without a bank account is an undesirable one, and the idea preposterous that he should be—
thought willing to share in any enterprise which predicts more benefit to the country than to himself, although he beholds every day this magnificent city, created from capital parted with at high interests, but parted with anyhow, while he will lend money at rather seven per cent. per annum, but on collaterals seven times the value which nobody has got. He at last returns to Europe, taking his money with him, but from sudden change of climate dies soon after in acute pain, or of apoplexy, leaving his money in the probate court, and not a dollar to the emigration fund.

Again, returning to our Borneo. The condition of the many millions who inhabit all Malaysia is deplorable and pitiful in the extreme. They are often barbarous. However, a single settlement like ours, sheltered by a naval station, will at once silence their piratical propensities, without we be called upon to appeal to the ships of war for actual interference, or a very formidable display of our strength as a nation. We can therefore set to work at once, and inasmuch as the lands of the company are worth but little if not settled upon, in comparison with California in 1849 so the overpopulated cities of the East will go there en masse. They will go and return *via* San Francisco. We here will receive everything produced in Borneo, *en route* for New York, and ship most of our manufactures to them from here. To California, especially San Francisco, this gigantic enterprise is of equally stupendous importance. All our manufacturers are benefitted by a new and daily increasing strictly additional market, at a steamer distance of four weeks; an entirely new market to what we had before. We are not so isolated any more at this endpole of the civilized world, in a large commercial point of view, if we admit that Asia is more important to all Europe, the former having double the population of the latter.

The unparalleled success in a war of 10 days between
Prussia and Austria, has demonstrated that the effect of
art in the perfection of the manufacture of destructive wea-
pons and armaments to kill and destroy, is now so great
that the most eager pagans for bloodshed will, and must,
henceforth give way to the policy of peace, so that the
most powerful of non-republican and non-free nations
throughout the universe will have at once to notice, that
their false strength of physical and social, instead of intellectual, superiority over one another, gives way beneath
their thrones and actual card-house fabrics; that the cla-
mor for freedom will press to the surface, and like a fear-
ful earthquake, will bring these time abused towers of
fictitious strength to the ground. If you then perceive the
huge odd-pile of debris, the masons of freedom will carry
enough off to America, that the remainder there will be
brotherly linked together, and grace a plateau life of men
equal before the law, a true copy of the glorious institutions
in our own, the mother land of freedom.

Then, and only then, will the world uplift their eyes in
exquisite thanks to God on high; they then, like we, and
only then, will bask in the sunshine of the day like the
violet or the oak, the snow drop of the arctic or the banian
tree of the tropics; the small intellect or the vast, the
shepherd or the lawyer, the yellow or the colors of the rain-
bow of mankind; a general leveling of every prejudice
lurking about from ignorance as to one man being superior
to another in the eyes of God, the father of all, except in
his mirror-clear conscience, known to him only, in his
love of fellowship, of disinterestedness, and of positive usefulness, through his own individual labor. This clue we
take from our physical organization to be obliged to
assuage the cravings of hunger and of thirst every four hours,
that when bodily satisfied our mind takes its share of labor,
which is civilization; and again, when darkness of night
sets regularly in every twelve hours, God wishes us to rest unknown to ourselves, and shielded by himself only, from

both our physical and mental labors and exertions of the day.

Returning to our subject of a settlement in Borneo, we are there secure from interference on the part of Europe, the late successful outrooting of the last remnant of European feudal principles in our own country, having afforded to all nations a proof of the colossal power of the United States as a nation, which will forever be remembered, securing to us everlasting peace.

In conclusion, I beg to rivet the attention of the merchants of Front street, and others, of the directors of all our flour mills, of every farmer throughout the coast, and every ship builder up and down the coast, and at last, of every one domiciled with us and throughout the United States, to the fact that the three European colonies within the Asiatic tropics—the Dutch at Batavia, the English at Singapore, and the Spanish at Manila, being within a week's reach from Borneo, the center, will henceforth become additional and entirely new customers of ours for the consumption of flour, to what we have this day in our schedules of demand from San Francisco for export; which flour said nations cannot do without, no more than we this day can do without their spices; and which flour, again, they cannot obtain from anywhere nearer than San Francisco, we being the nearest port of the temperate zone producing wheat; and furthermore, that this additional and new gain constitutes such vast quantities of flour, to be supplied permanently, as to become of the most vital importance to all our States on the Pacific coast to avail themselves of the new Borneo market; and positively demands the most energetic action on the part of our Chamber of Commerce, to without delay establish branch houses in Borneo for the sale of said vast quantities of flour, to unhesitatingly secure the trade.

Another most important consequence to California of an henceforth additional consumption of flour, to an extent barely computable, will be the provision for tonnage. Our coast will resound with the busy hum of the ship carpenter, and draw to the Bay the airy pinions of our majestic forests. We will be the first to draw from the banks of the picturesque river Knitchpeck, the material to cement together in everlasting friendship, the blending snows of Alaska with the evergreen foliage of the tropics of our Borneo.

For want of tonnage the farmer was scantily paid for his wheat, the mills checked in their energy, and the shipping merchant, through scarce tonnage and high freights, retarded in his enterprise. The meridians of our California lay bare for millions of acres east, for want of population to sow them over with cereals. Therefore, to lift the vail of Asia, with its 600,000,000 of people, and to behold our future so steady and lucrative in its development, we will in less than one hundred years outrival New York, which has but 300,000,000 opposite to trade with.

Thus the eagle of Liberty soars high above the Capitol of Washington. His flight is quick, and nothing escapes his vision. Thus Webster understood "the Union forever." His photograph and name I myself deposited in a station on the Desert of Egypt twelve years ago, and at Shepard's Hotel, Cairo. I planted a twig from our Tree of Liberty, where not a blade of grass will grow.

I advise any one whom years of success made, perhaps, thoughtless of the blessings of Freedom enjoyed with us, to travel outside of the United States, and he will quickly return, made miserable every where, and be happy only here at home. He will have learned that liberty, being the light of the soul, is a dowry from heaven, and does not belong to him and the United States only, but to the world at large; that it is his duty to devote his labor to the commonwealth and not all to his only self.

www.ingramcontent.com/pod-product-compliance
Lightning Source LLC
Chambersburg PA
CBHW021429090426
42739CB00009B/1416